LIANA PAREDES AREND
HILLWOOD MUSEUM AND GARDENS
WASHINGTON, D.C.

SÈVRES PORCELAIN

AT HILLWOOD

Library of Congress Cataloging-in-Publication Data
Arend, Liana Paredes, 1961–
    Sèvres porcelain at Hillwood / Liana Paredes Arend.
      p. cm. — (The Hillwood collection series)
    Includes bibliographical references.
    ISBN 0-9654958-5-X (pbk.)
      1. Sèvres porcelain. 2. Post, Marjorie Merriweather—Art collections.
3. Porcelain—Private collections—Washington (D.C.) 4. Porcelain—Washington (D.C.)
5. Hillwood Museum and Gardens. I. Hillwood Museum and Gardens. II. Title. III. Series.
    NK4390.A74   1998
    738.2'0944'074753—dc21   98-9972
                                       CIP
ISBN 0-9654958-5-X

Photographer: EDWARD OWEN
Editor: NANCY EICKEL
Designer: POLLY FRANCHINE, PRIMARYDESIGN
Printer: SCHNEIDEREITH AND SONS

Cover: TRAY FOR SOUP TUREEN (detail of fig. 54, p. 78)

Frontispiece: Fig. 1. These fantastic birds, painted by Philippe Castel, are from a garniture of three cuvettes "Courteille" (detail of fig. 40, p. 63).

Pages 2–3: CONDIMENT DISHES *(salières à trois compartiments),* (detail of fig. 5, p. 13)

Contents

Foreword

ONE OF THE GREATEST HOLDINGS IN THE EXPANSIVE collections at Hillwood is its large number of Sèvres porcelain. Pieces range from examples of the early years of the factory at Vincennes to a grand selection of eighteenth-century Sèvres pieces, including some outstanding vases as well as tablewares from celebrated services. Following the tradition of many wealthy American families in the first half of the twentieth century, Marjorie Merriweather Post strived to possess magnificent examples of eighteenth-century French furnishings and luxury arts, which were then considered the epitome of fine craftsmanship.

In the early 1920s Mrs. Post was tutored by the international art dealer Sir Joseph Duveen to appreciate fully the best qualities of the fine and decorative arts. She and her second husband, Edward F. Hutton, had built the largest triplex apartment in New York City. The architectural style of its handsome interior were of the Louis XV and Louis XVI periods. To embellish her home's impressive rooms, she amassed one of the finest collections of eighteenth-century French furniture in the United States. In addition, she began collecting early examples of soft-paste Sèvres as well as fine later pieces of hard-paste porcelain. Today, displayed in her last great residence at Hillwood, her Sèvres collection remains one of the most important in America.

The author of this excellent overview of Mrs. Post's Sèvres collection is Liana Paredes Arend, Hillwood's Curator of Western European Art. She has a profound knowledge of European decorative arts and has written extensively on various aspects of the Hillwood collection. Her outstanding contribution provides new insights into this superb collection.

This book is part of a growing series on the multifaceted Hillwood collection. I am grateful to the Board of Directors of the Marjorie Merriweather Post Foundation of D.C., which has supported this significant endeavor.

FREDERICK J. FISHER, DIRECTOR

FIG. 2
Vincennes soup tureen designed by Jean-Claude Duplessis (detail of fig. 8, p. 18)

Introduction

THE PORCELAIN FACTORY AT SÈVRES HAS BEEN IN EXISTENCE for two-and-a-half centuries. Since its beginning—first at Vincennes, then at Sèvres—the factory has produced some of the finest porcelain in Europe. The period represented by the objects in the Hillwood collection spans the early years of the manufacture at Vincennes to the time of the French Revolution. A few, but spectacular, examples cross the threshold into the nineteenth century to the period of the restoration of the Bourbon monarchy after the defeat of Napoleon.

No porcelain factory in eighteenth-century Europe reflected courtly taste better than Sèvres. The form and color of its pieces expressed the frivolity and the sheer joy of life of the privileged in the non-egalitarian society of the Ancien Régime. Assimilating this unashamedly aristocratic style often requires great effort on the part of viewers today. Sèvres certainly defies bourgeois and democratic taste. Contemporary notions of design and style must be put aside when embarking on a trip to the removed world of eighteenth-century aristocratic France.

FIG. 3
Rococo gilding delineated in crimson against a pink ground on a sugar bowl (detail of fig. 9, p. 23)

SOON AFTER MARJORIE MERRIWEATHER POST (1887–1973) inherited her father's fortune in 1914, she began collecting French furniture, porcelain, tapestries, and gold boxes under the guidance of art dealer Sir Joseph Duveen. The motifs that initially prompted her to collect French works of art and particularly Sèvres had much to do with becoming accepted as a collector of refined and discerning taste. Indeed, Sèvres, the royal French porcelain *par excellence,* offered the visual complement to well-appointed rooms in the Louis XV and Louis XVI styles, which were regarded as the epitome of good taste. In the words of author Edith Wharton, "Good objects of art give a room its crowning touch of distinction. Their intrinsic beauty is hardly more valuable than their suggestion of a mellower civilization—of days when rich men were patrons of the 'arts of elegance' and when collecting beautiful objects was one of the obligations of noble leisure."[1] If the collection Mrs. Post amassed throughout her lifetime can be labeled as eclectic, her collection of Sèvres has an uncharacteristic homogeneity. Her choices in this area reflect her personal affinity for turquoise and pink wares, and a clear preference for soft-paste productions (fig. 5). (The few examples of hard-paste porcelain at Hillwood were collected later in her lifetime, some at the recommendation of her curator, Marvin C. Ross.) The group of Sèvres has the unmistakable imprint of Mrs. Post's taste for the classical and the beautifully crafted, which is what, above all, characterized her collecting.

Mrs. Post built her collection piecemeal, making individual purchases

FIG. 4
DINING TABLE AT HILLWOOD
Set with plates made for Cardinal Prince Louis de Rohan in 1771 (see fig. 15, p. 33)

throughout her life from a wide variety of sources, primarily through dealers and major auction houses in London, Paris, and New York. By studying the annotated bills in her own handwriting, it becomes evident that she was personally involved in each purchase and its price negotiations. Her collection placed great emphasis on utilitarian wares, representing a wide range of shapes and decorations. While much of her Sèvres collection was intended for display, she also acquired Sèvres, in particular tableware, for use when entertaining. Dining at Mrs. Post's evoked the grandeur of great banquets of the past. The lace-covered table displayed porcelain sets commissioned by royalty and aristocracy of the eighteenth and nineteenth centuries. A plethora of candles reflected on mirrored walls and their light glanced off sparkling table glass and silver. Massive floral arrangements added a note of color and freshness to the table settings (fig. 4). Although Mrs. Post's first recorded purchase of Sèvres occurred in 1923 (fig. 30), her early significant acquisitions date to 1928 and 1929, when she bought several objects from J. Rochelle Thomas in London, including a *déjeuner* (fig. 6) and a socketed cup and saucer (fig. 47).

Over the next fifteen years she did not acquire much Sèvres, but after World War II, Mrs. Post was able to focus again on her French collecting, and she continued to buy Sèvres porcelains. During a trip to London in 1945, she made substantial purchases of Sèvres. A year later, interested in acquiring more *bleu céleste* pieces for her table, she asked her husband, Joseph E. Davies, who was visiting London at the time, to inquire for her at J. Rochelle Thomas, where she had bought several pieces of Sèvres the previous year. After trying to find the shop, Mr. Davies wrote a letter to his

FIG. 5
CONDIMENT DISHES
(*salières à trois compartiments*)
Pink (24.103.1–.2) marked with crossed letters
L, date letter Y for 1776,
and mark of painter Etienne Evans
Turquoise (24.28.1–.2) marked with crossed
letters L, ca. 1770
Each H. 3½ in. (9 cm)

FIG. 6
TEA OR COFFEE SERVICE
(*déjeuner "losange"*), ca. 1775
Each piece marked with crossed letters L
Tray L. 13¾ in. (35 cm); creamer H. 3¹⁵/₁₆ in.
(10 cm); cup H. 2³/₁₆ in. (6 cm);
saucer Dia. 5¼ in. (13.5 cm); 24.147.1–.6

wife, saying, "They cannot be located. Eleanor [Mrs. Post's second daughter] and I have exhausted all possibilities. They were bombed out."[2]

On this same trip to London, Mrs. Post's daughter did find a set of plates with blue borders, floral decoration, and distinctive hatched panels on gilt frames (fig. 51) at the Antique Porcelain Company. Mr. Weinberg, the owner of the shop, wanted to sell the entire service, insisting that it should not be split. Mrs. Post's intention to use the porcelain at her dining table is made clear in a letter of response. "About twenty-five years ago I acquired quite an extensive turquoise blue service, and it would, I am sure you would agree, be useless to duplicate things already owned. This service is one that we use. It is not for cabinet purposes. . . . The plates almost match exactly eighteen that I have; hence the twelve makes up my number of thirty for table service. . . ."[3] In this same light, her purchase of thirty plates from the Cardinal Prince Louis de Rohan Service is significant because it reflects her intention to use them at her dining room table (fig. 4). She acquired the Rohan plates from French and Company in New York, an interior design firm that Mrs. Post hired over the years to assist in decorating her residences. From French and Company she also purchased an outstanding turquoise blue tureen and platter in 1952 (fig. 8).

In 1949, coinciding with her role as a leading hostess of Washington high society, Marjorie Post Davies resumed her purchases of Sèvres by buying mainly from London dealers and auction houses. She bought the majority of the Morgan Service in 1949 from J. Rochelle Thomas (fig. 55). Aware that additional pieces had been dispersed at the J. P. Morgan sale (held at Christie's, London, on 29 March 1944), she persisted with the dealer in acquiring the rest of the pieces as they became available. In 1962 she had the opportunity to purchase the remaining pieces. A letter from the dealer put an end to the search: "As far as I know this is all there is remaining of this service and I do not contemplate finding more." The list of purchases made in 1949 includes many utilitarian wares, as well as the pair of draped vases (fig. 42) she acquired at Sotheby's (30–31 May) from the collection of Sir Bernard Eckstein, who a year earlier had bequeathed part of his large collection of Sèvres to the British Museum.

Some extraordinary utilitarian and ornamental wares were purchased in 1949. Two soup tureens and platters (figs. 53, 54) have a curious reunion history. They were not bought as a pair. Mrs. Post acquired the tureens in a Paris shop in 1949 and one of the platters from another shop in the city. Visiting Paris a year later, "Mrs. Davies spied the [other] platter in [a] shop . . . and pounced on it. [She] could not stand her luck when she found the platter."[4] Her purchase of the garniture of three *cuvettes "Courteille,"* one of the very few complete sets of this kind, dates to 1949 as well (fig. 40).

When Mrs. Post bought Hillwood in 1955 and proceeded to remodel and furnish her new magnificent residence in the heart of Washington, D.C., she had already thought of it as a place to display her collections. Thus, in 1956 and 1957 she acquired still more pieces of Sèvres to fill the porcelain foyer and the drawing room cases that she devoted to showing the royal French porcelains.

In the 1960s her curator, Marvin C. Ross, advised her in the purchase of several major pieces of Sèvres. Under his guidance she acquired the *cuvette "Mahon"* (fig. 7) at the sale of the René Fribourg collection at

FIG. 7
VASE
(cuvette "Mahon")
Marked with crossed letters *L* enclosing date letter *E* for 1757,
and mark of painter Philippe Parpette
H. 8⅛ in. (21.5 cm), L. 11½ in. (29 cm); 24.91

Sotheby's in London (4 May 1965). She also took his advice and success-fully bid on the vase with African birds at the Parke-Bernet sale of 19 January 1963 (fig. 65). Although Mrs. Post paid high prices for some items in her collection, she was generally very conscious about cost. When Mr. Weinberg from the Antique Porcelain Company offered a pair of rare 1760 pink pot-pourri vases with chinoiserie painting by Charles-Nicolas Dodin for a discounted price of $240,000, she politely, though sarcastically, replied, "The price for the two magnificent Sèvres vases is much too high even with the liberal discount you offer. I would not think of paying such a price unless they were mounted in jewels!"[5]

The collection of Sèvres assembled by Mrs. Post cannot claim to rival those found in major museums, nor was it gathered with the intention of presenting an illustrated history of the factory's productions. Instead, the Hillwood collection restores Sèvres to the position it held in eighteenth-century interiors—as a visual complement to elegantly decorated spaces.

FIG. 8
TUREEN AND PLATTER
(pot à oille "du roi" et son plateau)
Tureen marked with crossed letters *L* enclosing date letter *B* for 1754 and *G* (in script),
possibly for Jean-Baptiste-Etienne Genest, head of painter's studio
Platter unmarked
Tureen H. 12½ in. (31.8 cm); platter L. 16¹⁵/₁₆ in. (43 cm); 24.1–.3

THE SÈVRES MANUFACTORY

From Its Beginnings to the End of the Ancien Régime

IN THE EIGHTEENTH CENTURY THE PRODUCTION OF porcelain, such as it had been made in China since the seventh or eighth century, was the subject of fierce competition among many European countries. The commercial endeavors of the East India Companies in the seventeenth century led to an enormous influx of Oriental porcelain in Europe, which triggered a "chinamania" fad and a surge of European interest in discovering the secret recipe for porcelain. In the search for formulas to produce a glassy, impermeable, translucent, white ceramic body, porcelain manufacturing in Europe developed in two ways. The distinction is a purely technical one, expressed by the terms hard-paste and soft-paste porcelain. The Meissen factory, under the patronage of Augustus the Strong, elector of Saxony and king of Poland, was the first in Europe to make true (hard-paste) porcelain in 1709. Its formula successfully combined kaolin—the white clay indispensable to making hard-paste porcelain—with quartz feldspath. The mixture was fired at high temperatures (1250 to 1350 degrees centigrade), which resulted in a fusion of materials to form an impermeable, glassy ceramic body.

Deposits of kaolin were not found in France until 1768 in the area of Limoges. French factories countered this deficiency by multiplying their experiments and using other alternative ingredients in the hope of arriving at a material of similar impermeability and translucency. Their alternative formula is generically known as soft-paste porcelain. This paste, laboriously prepared from a wide variety of materials (mainly white clay, sand, and ground glass), was fired at a lower temperature (approximately 1200 degrees centigrade). Once a recipe for soft paste was obtained, the news spread rapidly, despite the zealous efforts of factories to guard their formulas. Artisans ran away with these secret formulas and tried to capital-ize on their privileged knowledge. In this way several factories were born: Saint-Cloud (ca. 1700), Lille (ca. 1711), Chantilly (ca. 1725), Mennecy (ca. 1735), and Vincennes (ca. 1740).

The beginnings of the Vincennes-Sèvres porcelain works, which ulti-mately became the celebrated *Manufacture royale de porcelaine* (Royal Manufactory of Porcelain), differed from the creation of many other porcelain manufactories throughout Europe. It did not start under royal or even noble patronage; instead it was established with the support of financiers and bankers.

The story of the creation of the Vincennes-Sèvres factory began in 1738, when the brothers Robert and Gilles Dubois, two artisans fleeing from Chantilly, took refuge with the keeper of the château de Vincennes. There they were introduced to Jean-Louis Orry de Fulvy, state counselor, financial superintendent, and director of the French East India Trade Company. Orry de Fulvy must have been involved with porcelain, and he most likely was interested in starting his own porcelain works. The Dubois brothers' arrival in Vincennes might have seemed a godsend, because they claimed to have the secret of making porcelain. On hearing this, Orry de Fulvy, through the influence of his brother, the powerful *contrôleur général des finances* Orry de Vignory, secured lodgings and workspace for the Dubois brothers at the old royal château de Vincennes and immediately supplied them with all the material they needed to proceed. At their evi-dent failure to make porcelain, Orry de Fulvy grew impatient, and the Dubois brothers resorted to calling their friend Louis-François Gravant from Chantilly with the hope that he could help. Gravant, offered the ben-efit of the doubt, was granted a little more time to work on a recipe. In due time, the workshop at Vincennes was the first to manufacture a clay of perfect whiteness and a porcelain with a fine translucent glaze on which the fame of the Vincennes-Sèvres venture still rests.

In 1745 a private company under the name of Charles Adam *(valet de chambre* to Orry de Fulvy) was created under the auspices of the crown and granted the exclusive twenty-year privilege of making porcelain "in the Saxon manner" (that is, with painted figures and gilding). At this same time others were expressly forbidden to produce porcelain of this specific kind. These privileges, disputed until the French Revolution of 1789, created constant friction with emerging porcelain factories in Paris.

To compete with Meissen, the best talent was brought to work at the factory in Vincennes. Easel painters, fan painters, and porcelain painters from Saint-Cloud and Chantilly were lured to join the new enterprise, which from 1751 counted the king among its shareholders. Soon workers at Vincennes moved beyond derivative interpretations of Oriental and Meissen porcelains to formulate a distinctive style of their own. The transition was accelerated by the appointment of Jean-Jacques Bachelier as artistic director in 1751. Under his supervision, the use of brightly colored grounds, combined with areas of white reserved for polychrome painting, and the lavish application of gilding to frame these areas became the factory's hallmark, imparting a uniquely French character to the production. This stylistic development should be seen in the context of a calculated move to compete with the appealing colors of Meissen porcelain. One Monsieur Hulst, who was employed to advise in matters of taste, must have had much to do with stylistic changes as well. In a letter to the director Jacques-René Boileau dated 21 September 1751, Hulst indicated that the main goal of the factory should be to "avoid the heavily decorated and the ordinary, and strive instead for lightness, refinement, novelty" and concluded that porcelain should call to mind "a pretty woman, smiling and agreeable."[6] Jean-Claude Duplessis, an Italian designer and silversmith who worked for the duke of Savoy, became the chief designer sometime around 1748. Some of the most satisfactory statements of French rococo are found in the forms Duplessis designed for the factory (figs. 7, 8). Jean Hellot, a member of the French Academy of Sciences, was hired to supervise the composition of the paste and the development of pigments to be used on the porcelain.

Despite its initial successes, Vincennes was in financial trouble by 1751. At this point it seemed crucial, if the enterprise were to survive, to gain the personal interest of King Louis XV. The next year the old company was dissolved, and a new company was established under the name of Eloy Brichard (a future *fermier-général*) in which the king owned a quarter of the shares. In August 1753 the factory became officially known as the *Manufacture du roi* and, in keeping with a practice that had begun some years earlier, was given the right to use the royal cipher of two interlaced letters *L* as its mark. From then on, a date letter was simply incorporated with the mark, that is, successive letters for successive years: *A* for 1753, *B* for 1754, and so on. When the alphabet ran out, letters were doubled—*AA* for 1778, *BB* for 1779—until *PP* for 1793, the year in which the royal cipher was substituted by *R. F.* for Republique Française. Next to the cipher painters and gilders frequently added their marks, which often consisted of a small symbol or their initials (see appendix). Very few pieces, however, have the ideal, picture-perfect set of marks. In principle, this fact should not be regarded with suspicion. Most pieces also carry incised marks, which were scratched into the paste before it was fired. These marks might correspond to the person who turned, molded, repaired, or trimmed the piece.

Coinciding with the institution of a marking system, a decision was made to transfer the factory from Vincennes to Sèvres. As a lover of porce-

FIG. 9
TEA OR COFFEE SERVICE
(cabaret), ca. 1758
Four cups and saucers, teapot, and sugar bowl each marked with crossed letters *L*
and mark of painter Vincent Taillandier; 24.94

lain and a great patron of the factory, Madame de Pompadour, mistress to Louis XV, has been credited as the principal advocate of the move from Vincennes to Sèvres, located west of Paris and closer to Versailles. The new building took three years to complete, and the factory was officially established at Sèvres in 1756. The move did not result in any great changes in style (fig. 9). Production continued without major interruption until the company fell into debt once more in 1759. This time the king paid all the debts and became the sole owner of the factory, an act that guaranteed its financial stability and boosted sales. The creation of the *porcelaine de France,* as it was known then, must be considered in serious social and economic terms. France imported Oriental and Meissen porcelains in great quantities, yet economic reasons and nationalistic pride dictated that France not only meet its own demand for porcelain but also become a major supplier in the export market. In addition, a strong porcelain industry in France would employ hundreds of qualified artisans. In keeping with the programmatic organization of the luxury art industries as instituted during the reign of Louis XIV, Louis XV, the king's great-grandson, patronized Sèvres. His continued support allowed Sèvres to play a main role as a trend-setting porcelain factory that would lend prestige both to the luxury arts and to the monarch himself.

The goal of becoming a serious competitor in the manufacture of porcelain nevertheless encountered numerous obstacles. The market was flooded with Oriental porcelains ranging from cheap to precious. Meissen

Fig. 10
Continuous vitruvian scroll border interspersed with pink harebells, from a tray (detail of fig. 41, p. 64)

porcelains also had been pouring into the French market since 1709, and the factory had endeavored to corner this lucrative market. Arriving late into this fierce competition, the soft-paste porcelain made at Sèvres was far more costly and difficult to produce. It was not as flexible or malleable as hard paste, and it warped and broke easily during firing. Kiln losses were so high that at the beginning it became almost impossible for the factory to make a profit. Despite these shortcomings, and thanks to the tenacity of entrepreneurs, the support of the crown, and the artistic talent of workers such as Duplessis, Bachelier, and Hellot, these obstacles were eventually overcome. Sèvres, along with Meissen, soon became the most prestigious of all factories in the Western world.

The introduction of hard-paste porcelain in the early 1770s brought about the greatest change in the factory's organization since its establishment. A whole series of workshops was created, new kilns built, and a completely new range of colors developed (fig. 11). To distinguish hard-paste productions from soft-paste ones, the marking system incorporated the royal crown surmounting the king's cipher.

The accession of Louis XVI to the throne in 1774 coincided with a period of creative and financial crisis at the factory due in great part to the competition of other Parisian porcelain factories that produced wares at much lower prices. Thanks to the discovery of kaolin, factories proliferated under the auspices of other members of the royal family: Manufacture de Monsieur (comte de Provence) at the rue de Clignancourt;

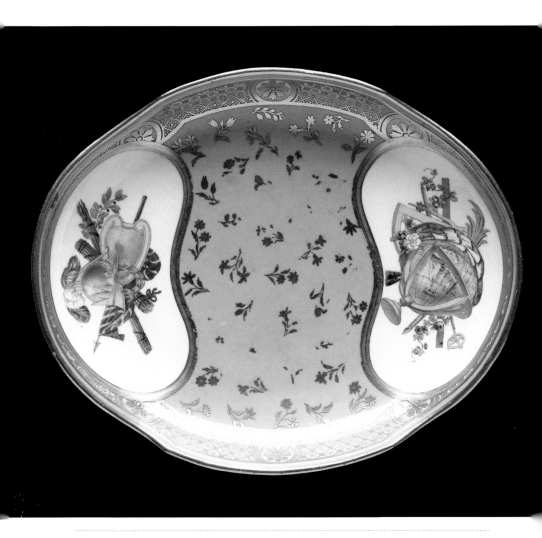

FIG. 11
TRAY
(jatte)
Marked with crossed letters *L* enclosing date letter *V* for 1774, surmounted by a crown indicating
hard-paste porcelain, and mark of painter Charles-Nicolas Buteux *l'aîné*
L. 9⅛ in. (23 cm); 24.150

Manufacture du comte d'Artois at the Faubourg Saint-Denis; Manufacture de la Reine on the rue Thiroux; Manufacture du duc d'Angoulême (Dihl & Gérard); and Manufacture du duc d'Orléans on the rue Amelot, to name a few. To overcome such competition, Sèvres productions became even more sumptuous. In 1782 the energetic comte d'Angivillier, who as *directeur des bâtiments* was also responsible for overseeing the functioning of the Sèvres factory, said with confidence, "French porcelain has placed French workmanship in the highest ranking position among all European courts. Chinese porcelain has lost the exclusive superiority that it enjoyed in this kingdom, which was the cause of our ruin and shame."[7]

SÈVRES PORCELAIN REFLECTED A LARGER SOCIOECONOMICAL trend that endeavored to create uniquely French styles. Indeed, the king's role as sole owner of the porcelain works contributed largely to the success of Sèvres. A man who dabbled in chemistry and enjoyed making things with his hands, the king must have been fascinated by the problems and processes of fabricating porcelain. He visited the factory frequently and took great interest in how it functioned. To show off the creations of Sèvres, Louis XV, and later Louis XVI, set up a Sèvres sales center in his private apartments in Versailles. Of course, every proud courtier felt obliged to acquire something. These sales soon assumed the character of great court events. At the sale held at Versailles in 1758, the duc d'Orléans probably purchased the *cuvette "Mahon"* (figs. 7, 12) for which he paid *au comptant* (in cash): haggling over prices was not allowed in such a refined setting.

Madame de Pompadour, the king's mistress, appreciated the French porcelain industry's significance as a potential source of revenue and as a fund for cultural prestige. She also grasped the opportunity to keep the king enthralled with her through their shared interest in Sèvres, something that was particularly important to her at a time when her relationship with the king was changing. Over the years the marquise herself set an extraordinary example by spending huge sums on acquiring Vincennes and Sèvres wares. She even insisted that for a person of means "not to buy the porcelain of Sèvres was to prove oneself a bad citizen."[8]

FIG. 12
Cuvette "Mahon" (detail of fig. 7, p. 16)

The prestige of Sèvres, promoted by the court, soon spread beyond French borders. The king boosted the reputation of Sèvres by giving porcelain pieces as diplomatic gifts to foreign ambassadors when political alliances or peace treaties were signed. At the signing of the Treaty of Versailles, which put an end to the War of Independence in the United States in 1783, the Duke of Manchester, the English ambassador who had participated in the negotiations, received a box set with diamonds. His wife accepted a beautiful service of Sèvres porcelain. This extraordinarily large dinner and dessert service originally included eighteen *coquetiers* (fig. 13). The service cost 20,000 *livres*. Even though George III of England found this extravagant gift-giving distasteful, Manchester approached the king for a reciprocal gift to present to the wife of the French foreign minister. The prime minister, the Duke of Portland, later described the king's reaction. "I will tell you in confidence that his majesty expresses his particular reluctance at being obliged to make these presents. . . . His wish is that the presents to each of the Ambassadors and Monsieur de Vergennes should not exceed 1,000 *livres* each."[9] Another example of this extravagant gift-giving is a service that Louis XVI presented to Archduke Ferdinand Karl of Austria, older brother of Marie Antoinette, in 1786. Beyond a sauce boat (fig. 14), few elements of this 280-piece service (intended for twenty-four to twenty-eight people) are extant. The service was dispersed at the sale of the belongings of Princess Paley (morganatic wife of Grand Duke Paul of Russia, uncle of Emperor Nicholas II) when it was removed from the Paley palace at Tsarskoe Selo (sold by Christie's, London, on 6 June 1929).

Princes, ambassadors, and aristocrats throughout Europe returned to their homelands laden with Sèvres. Coinciding with his appointment as ambassador to the court of Vienna, Cardinal Prince Louis de Rohan commissioned an elaborate and extremely expensive turquoise blue service decorated with his initials in two tones of gold and with paintings of birds in the reserves (fig. 15). Rohan is primarily remembered for his role in the celebrated affair of Marie Antoinette's diamond necklace, which earned him the nickname *le cardinal collier*. This costly service suited to perfection the cardinal's grand manner, lavish entertaining, and scandalous behavior, which so displeased Austrian empress Maria Theresa that she commanded he be recalled to France.

Rulers themselves ordered porcelain directly from the factory. The most celebrated order for a service was placed by Catherine II of Russia. She commissioned the so-called Cameo Service, to be done in the "newest and best style . . . after models taken from the Antique with cameo reproduc-

FIG. 13
EGG CUPS FROM A SET OF SIX FROM THE MANCHESTER SERVICE
(coquetiers)
Marked with crossed letters *L* and date letters *ff* for 1783; some pieces bear marks of painter
Pierre Massy and gilder Pierre-Jean-Baptiste Vandé *fils*
H. 1¾ in. (4.5 cm); 24.62
*Louis XVI presented this service to the Duchess of Manchester in recognition of the diplomatic efforts of
her husband in the signing of the Treaty of Versailles.*

FIG. 14
SAUCE BOAT
(saucière à deux becs)
Marked with crossed letters *L* with date letter *HH* for 1786,
and mark of painter Edmé-François Bouillat *père*; L. 9¹/₁₆ in. (24.5 cm); 24.17
This sauce boat comes from a service offered by Louis XVI to Archduke Ferdinand Karl of Austria,
older brother of Queen Marie Antoinette.

[32]

FIG. 15
PLATE FROM THE CARDINAL PRINCE LOUIS DE ROHAN SERVICE
(assiette)
Marked with crossed letters *L* enclosing date letter *S* for 1771,
and mark of painter Antoine-Joseph Chappuis *l'aîné*
Dia. 9¾ in. (25 cm); 24.66.1

tions."[10] The laborious technical process needed for this service required several firings for the *bleu céleste* ground color, the thick, lavish gilding, and the layered paste cameos. Costs skyrocketed for this enormous dinner and dessert service, which included about 800 pieces, among them 116 ice cups (fig. 56).

Ambassadors posted in Paris also helped disseminate the French style as represented by Sèvres. Prince Bariatinskii, Russian ambassador to the court of Versailles, served as an intermediary in Catherine's commission of the Cameo Service. In fact, Bariatinskii's involvement in these dealings may have led him to commission his own Sèvres service (fig. 59). Other Russians, most notably the Iusupovs, who commissioned four large services, patronized the French factory as well.

The factory's prosperity was not due solely to royal ownership and promotion. It also depended greatly on purchases made by the fashionable Parisian dealers whose advice was sought on which shapes and decorations to produce. These *marchands-merciers,* or dealers in decorative arts, played key roles in spreading the taste for Sèvres. Essential middlemen, they were crucial as arbiters of taste who introduced new trends into the rapidly expanding market for decorative art objects. For those who wanted to be *au courant,* a visit to the *marchands-merciers* was *de rigueur.* Over the years large quantities of porcelain were sold to dealers, which they then used to create elaborate confections of mixed media. Combining Vincennes flowers with Oriental or Meissen figurines to create inkstands and candelabra (fig. 16) was a specialty of the dealer Lazare Duvaux. Such items as gilt

FIG. 16
GILT BRONZE AND PORCELAIN CANDELABRA
Meissen figures representing Harlequin and Columbine after models by J. J. Kaendler, ca. 1748;
ormolu branches fitted with a profusion of Vincennes flowers
H. 17½ in. (44.5 cm); 14.1.1–.2

FIG. 17
SÈVRES PLAQUE
One of three inserted into a marquetry table, ca. 1776; 31.25

FIG. 18
ORMOLU AND BISCUIT MANTEL CLOCK
Clock signed *Maniere, Paris;* Sèvres biscuit figures, ca. 1790,
inscribed *La Leçon de l'Amour* and *La Leçon à l'Amour*
H. 15½ in. (39.5 cm), L. 17 in. (43 cm); 16.2

bronze candelabra with Meissen figures and a profusion of Vincennes flowers are mentioned in his records. Porcelain plaques inserted into furniture
was an innovation introduced by the fashionable shopkeeper Simon-
Philippe Poirier, who, along with Dominique Daguerre, held the monop-
oly on such plaques. One porcelain plaque inserted into a marquetry table
at Hillwood retains a price sticker from the factory that indicates it cost
seventy-two *livres* (fig. 17). Two biscuit figures inserted into the clock case
signed by Manière attest to the use of Sèvres in furnishings as late as the
1790s (fig. 18).

TECHNICAL PROCESS AND COLOR PALETTE

SOFT-PASTE PORCELAIN POSSESSED A NUMBER OF SHORT-comings: it was difficult to prepare and fire, it was not very plastic, and it was not as hard or resistant to changes in temperature as was hard-paste porcelain. Its easily scratched, soft surface generated its name. Despite these inconveniences, soft paste offered certain advantages over hard paste: its ivory white body is more pleasant to the eye than the stony white of hard paste, and its lead glaze absorbs an unlimited number of colors beautifully. The range of alkaline colors formulated at Sèvres for use with soft paste has a wonderful depth. The gold sparkles due to its extraordinary shine and thickness. A piece of decorated soft-paste porcelain required at least four firings: first, the biscuit firing, which made the object hard as stone; then the lead glaze was fired on, followed by the painted decoration and finally the gilding. The losses in the firing process were so staggering that in the early years of Sèvres it became difficult to make a profit.

If this soft paste and its glaze were wonderful for utilitarian and orna-mental wares in general, they were not so good for sculpture. Glazed and painted sculpture had been produced at Vincennes since the late 1740s, but the final product could not match the quality of similar Meissen wares. The sculpture produced was clumsy, with details blurred by the viscous, pool-ing glaze. In 1749 Bachelier proposed to transform the shortcoming into a virtue simply by issuing finished statues in their biscuit state, that is, fired but not glazed. The surface of the unglazed porcelain was polished with a

FIG. 19
Gilding on Franklin cup (detail of fig. 34, p. 57)
The high relief of the gilding decoration results from the two or three layers of gold that were fired separately.
The fine tooling is the work of master gilder Etienne-Henry Le Guay.

sandstone abrasive to produce a soft, matte appearance much like the natural beauty of white marble sculpture (fig. 22).

The use of colored grounds also became a hallmark of Sèvres (fig. 20). Public appetite for vibrant colors marked a sharp departure from earlier productions, many of which had white grounds. By the mid-1750s extensive experimentation with colors resulted in the invention of some of the most famous ground colors, including dark blue *(bleu lapis)* before 1753, turquoise *(bleu céleste)* and yellow in 1753, green in 1756, and pink in 1757.

Bleu céleste or turquoise blue is also known as *bleu Hellot* after its inventor, Jean Hellot. The color referred to the *céleste Empire*—China—to describe a color similar to that of the bright turquoise glaze found on Chinese ceramics of the K'ang Hsi period (1662–1722).Turquoise was first used for tableware in Louis XV's service of 1753.The *pot à oille* at Hillwood (fig. 8) bears a date mark for 1754 and is one of the earliest and grandest examples of turquoise blue tableware. It may have formed part of the king's service, in which pieces were adorned with different patterns of decoration.The beautiful, cloudy, uneven quality but deep tone of the blue is one of its charms. The sculptural quality of the design attributed to Duplessis links it with the great service pieces created by Parisian silversmiths for the royal table.

The first formula for pink, or *roze,* dates from 1757, but no pieces with this ground color were actually produced until 1758. It has been argued that the main reason for this delay lay in the difficulties encountered in applying gold over the pink color. As a ground color, pink was preferred for decorative wares rather than for tablewares. Indeed, few services were

FIG. 20

Detail of ground decoration known as fond Taillandier (pointillé ground) on saucer (24.155.2)
in magenta, with white areas reserved to receive polychrome painting within gilt frames

made with a pink ground. On the pink ice cups in the Hillwood collection, part of a 1775 service of this color, the gilding obviously bled into the ground color (fig. 21). To better delineate the gilding from the ground, the gilding was often profiled with a line of darker pink or crimson (figs. 3, 23).

Occasionally, and for very short periods, colors were used in combinations: pink and green in 1758, some green and lapis blue in 1759, and pink and lapis in 1762 (fig. 23). Intricate patterns as well as solid colors were utilized for ground colors. In fact, patterned grounds became a distinctive feature of Sèvres wares. Among the most popular were pebbled, *caillouté*, fretwork *à la reine* in imitation of marquetry designs (fig. 31), "*oeil de perdrix*," *fond pointillé*, or *fond Taillandier* for Vincent Taillandier, the painter who created it (figs. 20, 24).

Gold, which was fired at the lowest temperature, had to be applied last.

FIG. 21
ICE CUPS
(tasses à glace) from a set of six
Variously marked with crossed letters *L*
enclosing date letter *X* for 1775, and marks of
gilders Charles-Nicolas Buteux *l'aîné*,
Théodore (Pierre-Théodore Buteux), and
Michel-Barnabé Chauvaux *l'aîné*
Each H. 2⅜ in. (6 cm); 24.101.1–.3

FIG. 22
STATUETTE OF HEBE
Biscuit porcelain, ca. 1770, with letter *B* incised
on base for Jean-Jacques Bachelier
H. 7½ in. (19 cm); 24.165
Modeled after marble sculpture of 1753
by Jacques-François-Joseph Saly

When the vogue for richly gilt pieces intensified, the factory's financial worries became more serious. The greater part of gold decoration was executed with a brush. To facilitate this step, the gold was ground to a fine powder, mixed with turpentine, and applied with a brush, just like regular painting. Two coats of gilding were usually applied to provide relief. When the gold was first fired, it lost its metallic sheen. Consequently it had to be partly polished and partly left matte, depending on the desired effect.

FIG. 23
TEA CADDY
(boîte à thé)
Marked with crossed letters *L* enclosing date
letter *K* for 1762
H. 3 in. (7.5 cm); 24.90.1–.2

FIG. 24
Landscape painting and pointillé ground
(fond Taillandier) on a dejeuner tray
(detail of fig. 6, p. 13)

FIG. 25
Back of flower vase from centerpiece of garniture of cuvettes "Courteille" (detail of fig. 40, p. 63)
A floral medallion, enclosed by a burnished and matte gold frame tooled with a neoclassical knot pattern, is the
work of gilder Henry-François Vincent le jeune.

Careful tooling to create a wide array of lively designs and thick applica-
tions of gold to give texture helped forge the fame of Sèvres gilding. They
are also one of the best ways to recognize imitations of Sèvres (fig. 19). The
earliest versions of gilding patterns are very rococo in spirit. They form
asymmetrical compositions (fig. 32) or consist of birds, trelliswork, palm
fronds, and/or flowers. Gilding became more restrained in the late 1750s,
with simple, wide lines tooled with repetitive patterns in contrasting matte
and burnished gold (fig. 25). Although yellow gold was used almost exclu-
sively, in 1771 yellow gold appears in combination with green gold in the
monogram of the Rohan Service (fig. 15).

For hard-paste porcelain three firings sufficed, in as much as its glaze
could be fixed in the first firing. Hard paste did not require as thick an
application of gold as did soft paste, and therefore it lent itself less readily
to elaborate tooling. This new material did not presuppose a decline in the
production of soft-paste porcelain, the taste for which prevailed among the
factory's clients. In fact, the soft-paste kilns were not closed until 1804.

DECORATIONS

THE EVOLUTION OF DECORATION AT SÈVRES IS NOT ALWAYS immediately apparent. Flowers, birds, trophies, and figure scenes are just as likely to be seen in porcelain dating from the 1760s as in pieces produced in the 1790s. Crucial to the development of porcelain design was Bachelier's role as director of the painter's atelier since 1748. He provided formal instruction to the painters, and in that respect he undoubtedly exercised an important influence on the decoration and style of porcelain at Sèvres, resulting in a factory "look." That painters might develop extraordinarily individual styles was not desirable since several artisans often worked together in decorating a large dinner service (figs. 51, 55). In small sets or single items, however, a painter's characteristic style might emerge. These decorators almost invariably specialized in a particular genre. Among them were Charles-Nicolas Dodin and Etienne-Jean Chabry, who painted figures in pastoral and mythological scenes (fig. 30), Jean-Louis Morin, who painted marine scenes (fig. 31), François-Joseph Aloncle and Etienne Evans, who concentrated on birds (fig. 58), and the virtuoso gilders Etienne-Henry Le Guay (figs. 19, 34) and Henry-François Vincent (figs. 25, 40, 53, 54).

Flowers were the most widely used decorative motif throughout the eighteenth century. Ranging from natural to fantastic, they were frequently arranged in bouquets and were sometimes combined with fruit (fig. 26). As the century progressed, the style of flower painting evolved towards a naturalism that reached its fullest expression in the flower painting found

FIG. 26
Flower painting showing a combination of flowers and fruit decorating a plate from 1768 (detail of fig. 51, p. 75)

on hard-paste soup tureens (fig. 27) and, on a smaller scale, on a yellow cup and saucer with flowers on a terrace (fig. 28).

Birds were another frequent subject. Early on representations of birds possessed a fantastic character, and they are seldom identifiable (fig. 29). The *Histoire naturelle des oiseaux* by Georges-Louis Leclerc, comte de Buffon, served as a main source of inspiration for bird painting. Many services with birds were produced at Sèvres using Buffon's encyclopedic compendium of ornithological species as a reference. Among these were Hillwood's yellow service with birds and "Etruscan" borders (fig. 58). In a scientific spirit, each piece is inscribed on the back with the name of the bird or birds represented on the front. A most uncommon but direct approach to bird painting was taken for the decoration of the *Oiseaux de l'Amérique Meridionale* Service in 1821. For that, Madame Knip, a painter of birds, accompanied Alexandre Brongniart, the director of the factory, to the

FIG. 27
Naturalistic flower painting attributed to Nicolas Sinsson, from a tray, ca. 1783 (detail of fig. 53, p. 78)

Musée d'Histoire Naturelle, where they selected the birds to be painted from nature (figs. 62–64).

While painting on white reserves framed with gold against a colored background became a distinctive characteristic of the earliest productions at Sèvres, figural scenes and landscapes that filled the whole cartouche distinguished many pieces created soon thereafter (figs. 24, 30). Out of the wide array of subjects proposed as decorations, many derived from printed sources. Sèvres painters had at their disposal numerous engravings,

FIG. 28
CUP AND SAUCER WITH FLOWERS ON TERRACE
(gobelet "litron" et soucoupe)
Marked with crossed letters *L* enclosing date letter *CC* for 1780,
and marks of painter Nicolas Sinsson and gilder Henry-François Vincent *le jeune*
Cup H. 2¾ in. (7 cm); saucer Dia. 5¹⁵/₁₆ in. (13.5 cm); 24.123.1–.2

drawings, and even paintings from which to copy. Figure painting, their exclusive right through the royal privilege received in 1745, was popular from the beginning. The famed artist François Boucher had collaborated with factory painters since the early days of Sèvres. His lighthearted compositions with cupids and pastoral scenes, so highly favored by Madame de Pompadour, enlivened Sèvres porcelain. In addition to the numerous engravings made after his paintings, factory records show that Boucher

FIG. 29
ICE CUPS FROM THE CARDINAL PRINCE LOUIS DE ROHAN SERVICE
(tasses à glace)
Variously marked with crossed letters *L,* date letter *S* for 1771,
and marks of painter Antoine-Joseph Chappuis *aîné* and painter and gilder Fallot
Each H. 2 9/16 in. (6.5 cm); 24.65

FIG. 30
COVERED CUP AND SAUCER WITH TRAY
(ecuelle et son plateau)
Marked with crossed letters *L* enclosing date letter *X* for 1775,
and mark of painter Etienne-Jean Chabry *fils*
Bowl Dia. 5⅛ in. (13 cm); tray L. 8⅞ in. (22 cm); 24.18.1–.3

himself received payments for supplying paintings and drawings for use by staff artists. Scenes on the saucer of the turquoise blue *ecuelle* (fig. 30) derive from two engravings by G. Demarteau after Boucher entitled *Les amants surpris* and *La pipée*. Demarteau also engraved the scene of a boy and his dog that decorates the lid of the *ecuelle* after Jean-Baptiste Huet's composition of 1770. These original and contemporary French scenes greatly appealed to factory clients, as did seventeenth-century genre scenes after the Flemish painters David Teniers the Younger and Philip Wouwermans, which were in line with the informal lifestyle that the king and his court privately enjoyed. Dock scenes, a genre in which Morin specialized (fig. 31), were recurrent, although rarely can a canvas or print be cited as an actual source.

FIG. 31
CUP AND SAUCER
WITH MARINE SCENES
(gobelet "litron" et soucoupe), ca. 1765
Marked with crossed letters *L*;
painting attributed to Jean-Louis Morin
Cup H. 3 in. (7.5 cm);
saucer Dia. 5⅞ in. (15 cm); 24.39.1–.2

FIG. 32
Pastoral motif from a tray
Painting attributed to Nicolas Sinsson, ca. 1783
(detail of fig. 53, p. 79)

Pastoral themes, a more feminine interpretation of neoclassicism, became prominent in Sèvres decorations. Clusters of elements of pastoral life (fig. 32), triumphs, and allegorical references to the arts, sciences, and military powers (fig. 11), suspended from ribbons (fig. 7), commonly decorate porcelains from the 1770s. Military conflicts waged during the eighteenth century also left their mark on porcelain. At first sight the courteous and graceful features of eighteenth-century art might convey the impression that this was a tranquil, peaceful era, but in fact scarcely a decade elapsed without war. Encampment scenes reflect the pervasive military atmosphere of this period, yet they can scarcely be connected to a particular event. Rather than represent the horrors of war, such images show pleasant snapshots of military life suitable to the beautiful decorative aspect of the porcelain (fig. 33).

Commemorative pieces were produced to highlight historical events. To honor the signing of the treaties of Amity, Commerce, and Alliance between France and the United States, several cups and saucers were issued in 1779 featuring the portrait of Benjamin Franklin, the American envoy to Versailles during the American War of Independence (fig. 34). An instrumental figure in securing France's recognition of American independence, Franklin became so popularly regarded as an apostle of liberty that his likeness appeared in all kinds of media. Mobbed wherever he went in Paris, Franklin wrote to his daughter in June 1779 that all these likenesses "have made your father's face as well known as the moon. . . . From the number of *dolls* now made of him he may be truly said to be *i-doll-ized* in this country."[11]

The factory's constant search for novel types of decoration and for a wider range of colors is apparent in the assorted cups and saucers at Hillwood. In decorating cups and saucers intended for display, the porcelain painters, free from the constraints of following particular patterns, felt at ease to express themselves as artists. Peculiar to production in the late 1780s are rebus cups and saucers. Intended as witty, devotional gifts to a lady from her lover or admirer, they are painted with thinly veiled messages of love and admiration (fig. 35). A small *gobelet "litron"* bears fragmentary, synthesized plant forms and geometric shapes that reflect a close link with contemporary silk patterns (fig. 36), while a few others have essentially abstract decorative patterns (fig. 46). Shortly after Jean-Jacques Langrenée *le jeune* assumed his official appointment as the factory's artistic co-director in 1785, he issued an array of arabesque designs that were to be repro-

duced in a whole line of porcelain creations. The rhythmical arrangement of delicate motifs to create the dreamlike "garden construction" seen on a cup and saucer (fig. 37) superbly illustrates the *style arabesque* at Sèvres. Together, the cups and saucers in the Hillwood collection can be interpreted as a microcosm of the variety of decorations found on Sèvres porcelain.

FIG. 35

PAIR OF REBUS CUPS AND SAUCERS

(gobelets "litron" et soucoupes)

Both marked with crossed letters *L* enclosing date letter *KK* for 1788,
an unidentified painter's mark *(V),* and mark attributed to gilder François Mirey
Each cup H. 2¹⁵/₁₆ in. (7.5 cm); each saucer Dia. 4⅝ in. (12 cm); 24.127.1–.4

FIG. 36

(right top)

CUP AND SAUCER WITH PALM FRONDS

(gobelet "litron" et soucoupe), ca. 1770

Unmarked; Cup H. 1⅜ in. (3.5 cm); saucer Dia. 4¼ in. (10.5 cm); 24.154.1–.2

FIG. 37

(right bottom)

CUP AND SAUCER WITH ARABESQUES

(gobelet "litron" et soucoupe)

Marked with crossed letters *L* and date letter *KK* for 1788,
and mark of painter Nicolas Dutanda and mark attributed to gilder François Mirey
Cup H. 1⅜ in (3.5 cm); saucer Dia. 4¼ in. (10.5 cm); 24.125.1–.2

ORNAMENTAL AND UTILITARIAN WARES

MANY OF THE FORMS PRODUCED AT SÈVRES WERE DESIGNED in the early years of the factory's existence and continued to be manufactured throughout the eighteenth and even into the nineteenth century.

Porcelain flowers brought the first commercial success to Vincennes (fig. 38). Made expressly for sale to *marchands-merciers,* these delicate flowers were incorporated into objects that were supplied as part of room decorations. They were arranged in vases, chandeliers, candelabra, or inkstands, and in some instances combined with porcelain figures (fig. 16). According to one well-known anecdote, Madame de Pompadour invited Louis XV to her château at Bellevue. There, she brought him into a garden in which all the flowers were made of porcelain and had been scented to create the illusion of natural flowers. In this same vein, the marquis d'Argenson, always informed of the latest gossip and scandal at court, reported in 1750 that "the king has ordered 80.000 *livres* worth of porcelain flowers from Vincennes, not only for his country homes but also for the château de Bellevue, residence of Madame de Pompadour. Everyone in Paris is talking about this, and frankly, this display of luxury has scandalized many."[12]

Sèvres is perhaps unequaled in the seemingly endless creative variety and sheer number of its vases. Although the Hillwood collection cannot boast the most elaborate types and variety of Sèvres vases, it does possess some outstanding pieces, ranging from voluptuous rococo fantasies to urn-like shapes from the neoclassical period. Vases could be utilitarian or purely ornamental. As early as 1753 pot-pourri vases were made at Sèvres to fight ever-present unpleasant odors. These containers for floral mixtures became indispensable objects in a luxury household. One type known as pot-pourri "*Pompadour*" is associated with the king's mistress, who was one of the factory's great promoters and clients. These urn-shaped pots, designed by Duplessis, are pierced at shoulder height with six holes to let

the fragrance of the flower petals and scented oils inside fill the room (fig. 39). Although virtually identical, the pots were made two years apart, the later one possibly ordered to pair with an earlier one or to replace a broken mate.

Many vases were intended to hold either porcelain flowers or real ones planted in soil. (Flowers were almost never set in fresh water, as we are accustomed to do today.) The *cuvette "Mahon"* (fig. 7), ascribed to the creative genius of Duplessis, could have held flowers or simply been used as an ornamental piece. With its bombé outline, shell-shaped sides, and scrolled feet, it is a vigorous rococo statement in French porcelain. Its name refers to the city of Mahon on the island of Minorca, which was captured by the French in 1756 and celebrated as one of the great triumphs during the Seven Years' War. ("Mahonaisse" sauce was also first served in com-

FIG. 38

Vincennes flowers set in ormolu branches of candelabra (detail of fig. 16, p. 35)

memoration of this victory.) The piece bears the date letter for 1757, an indication that it was one of the first pink wares ever produced. Almost certainly it is the very cuvette that the duc d'Orléans purchased from the king's sale at Versailles in December 1758.[13]

The factory was particularly reluctant to alter the shapes of its best-selling pieces. Such was the case of the *cuvette "Courteille,"* one of the classic shapes at Sèvres. Its restrained rococo decoration adapted so perfectly to a neoclassical design that it was produced in three sizes and used throughout the century (fig. 40). This set was intended for display on a commode, pier

table, or chimney piece as a *garniture de cheminée* before a mirror. Not only do the bird paintings on the front of each display high artistic quality and attention to detail (fig. 1), but the back of the vases are delicately decorated with floral medallions (fig. 25).

While unequivocally neoclassical shapes for vases became popular in the 1760s, decisively neoclassical motifs were produced at Sèvres as early as 1757. One of the earliest neoclassical statements at Sèvres is a rectangular tray known as a *plateau "tiroir" à jours* (fig. 41). Its openwork sides feature a continuous vitruvian scroll interspersed with stylized harebells (fig. 10). A pair of *vase "bouteille en écharpes,"* characterized by their slender form and tall, fluted necks and distinguished by the absence of patterned decoration, illustrate the classical design at its purest (fig. 42). These vases may have been intended to be fitted with mounts, as other comparable examples bear bronze mounts around the neck and base.

FIG. 40
GARNITURE OF THREE VASES
(cuvettes "Courteille")
Each marked with crossed letters *L* enclosing date letter *CC* for 1782,
surmounted by a crown indicating hard-paste porcelain,
and marks of painter Philippe Castel and gilder Henry-François Vincent *le jeune*
24.106.1: H. 7½ in. (19 cm), L. 11½ in. (29 cm)
24.106.2, 24.106.3: H. 6 in. (15 cm), L: 7⅞ in. (20 cm)

FIG. 41
TRAY WITH SIDES IN OPENWORK WITH VITRUVIAN SCROLL
(plateau "tiroir" à jours)
Marked with crossed letters *L* enclosing date letter *F* for 1758,
and with a mark attributed to painter Edmé Gomery
L. 9½ in. (24 cm), W. 6⅜ in. (17 cm); 24.93

FIG. 42
PAIR OF DRAPED VASES
(vases "bouteilles en écharpes" or flaçons "à mouchoirs"), ca. 1765
Unmarked
Each H. 10¼ in. (26 cm); 24.186.1–.4

In 1752 the factory began producing biscuit sculpture for sale. At the beginning, figural groups after designs by Boucher were very popular. Although the production of Boucher's groups continued throughout the eighteenth century, neoclassical models from the 1760s onwards reached a new artistic height. Etienne-Maurice Falconet brought a period of artistic renewal in the sculpture workshop from 1757 until he left for Russia nine years later. Bachelier replaced Falconet as director of sculpture until Simon Boizot was appointed director in 1773. The elaborate group of three scantily clad women carrying Cupid on their shoulders (fig. 43) relates to a design by Boucher entitled *Les Trois Graces portant l'Amour* and was included among the biscuit figures that complemented the Cameo Service made for Catherine II of Russia. *Hebe* (fig. 22), the cup bearer to the gods, was modeled after Jacques-François-Joseph Saly's sculpture that was exhibited at the Paris Salon of 1753. The two sculptures bear the incised letter *B,* which has been interpreted as Bachelier's signature while he was head of the Sèvres workshop (1766–73). The biscuit technique mastered at Sèvres helped to preserve the artist's crisp modeling and minute attention to detail, which was carried out by the *répareurs,* who refined the work before it was fired (fig. 44).

FIG. 43
GRACES AND CUPID
(*Les Trois Graces portant l'Amour*)
Biscuit porcelain, ca. 1770
Marked with letter *B* incised on base
for Jean-Jacques Bachelier
H. 10½ in. (26.5 cm); 24.166

FIG. 44
Modeling of biscuit figures
(*detail of fig. 43, p. 66*)

Among tableware, the greatest efforts in the first period of the factory's
history were concentrated on less ambitious forms, first and foremost on
cups and saucers (fig. 45), teapots, and sugar bowls. Vincennes established
models for cups and saucers that were used throughout the eighteenth and
nineteenth centuries. Original forms include the *gobelet "litron"* (cylindri-
cal in shape, with straight sides), the *gobelet "Hébert"* (pear shaped), and the
gobelet "Calabre" (curving slightly at the bottom), to name a few. The depth
and large size of the saucers can be explained by the fact that until the early
1780s, the polite custom for drinking coffee or tea was to pour the hot liq-
uid from the cup into the saucer to cool it off. As Abbé Cosson related to
his friend, Abbé Delille, when he was asked about coffee drinking with
courtiers at Versailles, "[I did] like everyone else: it was hot, and I poured it
little by little from the cup into the saucer."[14]

Usually cups and saucers matched other pieces of tea or coffee services,
but during the 1760s a vogue arose for collecting differently decorated
examples to form "Harlequin" sets, which were considered more appro-
priate for display than for use. The aunts of Louis XV were so proud of
their different Sèvres cups and saucers that they displayed them on two side
tables between windows in the winter salon of their château at Bellevue.[15]
During a visit to Paris in 1766, connoisseur Horace Walpole visited the
marchand-mercier Dulac's shop on the rue Saint-Honoré to make some purchases for his friend, the Reverend William Cole. Walpole later reported, "I
have executed your commission in a way that I hope will please you. As
you tell me you have a blue cup and saucer, and a red one, and would have
them completed to six, without all being alike, I have bought you one

(right top)
CUP AND SAUCER
(gobelet "Hébert" et soucoupe)
Marked with crossed letters L enclosing date letter A for 1753,
and mark of painter Vincent Taillandier
Cup H. 2⅝ in. (6.5 cm); saucer Dia. 5½ in. (14 cm); 24.37.1–.2

[68]

FIG. 46
"HARLEQUIN" SET OF CUPS AND SAUCERS
Left to right: (24.146.1–.2) Marked with crossed letters *L*, date letter *R* for 1770, and mark of painter
Louis-Jean Thévenet *père;* (24.145.1–.2) Marked with crossed letters *L* enclosing date letter *M* for
1765, and mark of painter and gilder Guillaume Noël; (24.148.1–.2) Unmarked, ca. 1770
Each cup H. 1¾ in. (4.5 cm); each saucer Dia. 4⅛ in. (10.5 cm)

other blue, one other red, and two decorated with sprigs" (fig. 46).[16]

A very peculiar model, consisting of a socketed cup and saucer, was introduced in 1759 (fig. 47). Contrary to popular belief, this shape was not described in factory records by the term *trembleuse,* nor was it necessarily intended for the elderly. (Marie Antoinette purchased one when she was eighteen.) Instead, the shape probably allowed the sick and ailing to get a better hold on the cup and saucer.

Covered broth basins with trays, called *ecuelles,* derived from silver prototypes (figs. 30, 48). They were not part of large dinner services but were

FIG. 47
SOCKETED CUP AND SAUCER
(gobelet couvert et soucoupe enfoncé)
Marked with crossed letters *L* enclosing date letter *aa* for 1778,
and mark of painter Philippe Castel
Cup H. 3⁷/₁₆ in. (8.5 cm); saucer Dia. 5¹⁵/₁₆ in. (15 cm); 24.158.1–.3

instead sold individually to be used for broths and soups that could be drunk in the intimacy of the bedroom or boudoir during the lengthy *toilette*. In her memoirs Madame de Sevigné recalled assisting to the toilette of the duchesse de Bourbon and watching during her hairdressing. The duchesse rose at noon, slipped into her gown, and ate bread and some soup while she combed her hair and powdered her face. *Ecuelles* were also customarily presented to nursing mothers, who were given specially rich and nutritious broths while they recovered from childbirth. The large plate held the accompanying bread.

FIG. 48
ROUND BOWL WITH COVER AND TRAY
(ecuelle et son plateau)
Marked with crossed letters *L* enclosing date letter *q* for 1769,
and mark of painter Pierre-Antoine Méreaud *l'aîné*
Cup H. 4½ in. (11.5 cm); tray L. 5⁵/₁₆ in. (13.5 cm); 24.133.1–.3

FIG. 49
TEA OR COFFEE SET WITH BELLFLOWERS
(déjeuner "losange")
Tray marked with crossed letters *L* enclosing date letter *O* for 1767,
and mark of painter Charles-Louis Méreaud *le jeune*
Tray L. 13¹¹/₁₆ in. (34 cm); saucer Dia. 5⅜ in. (13.5 cm); cup H. 2⅜ in. (6 cm); jug H. 4 in. (10 cm);
sugar bowl (cover missing) H. 1¹³/₁₆ in. (4.5 cm); teapot H. 4⅛ in. (10.5 cm); 24.132.1–.7

In later years *cabarets* consisting of a few coffee or tea service pieces assembled on lacquer or porcelain trays became a popular product (figs. 6, 9, 49). Tea was taken for pleasure and for its medicinal properties. The French drank tea everywhere: in bedrooms, boudoirs, salons, even in the bath. The small size of the teapots may be explained by the fact that the pot contained a concentrated brew that was diluted in water just before drinking. The decoration of a *déjeuner "losange"*—blue and purple bellflowers on a stippled *(sablé)* gold ground (fig. 50)—was the specialty of the painter Charles-Louis Méreaud, an artist who routinely painted flowers, nosegays, and garlands.

FIG. 50
Border of tray with bellflowers on a sablé (stippled) ground (detail of fig. 49, p. 72)

TABLEWARES AND DINING HABITS

In Eighteenth-Century France

QUANTITATIVELY, TABLEWARES ACCOUNT FOR THE MAJORITY of the production at Sèvres. The unity of design in tablewares is an eighteenth-century phenomenon. Before, table services were not part of a unified ensemble adhering to the same decorative pattern. Not until the reign of Louis XV were table services conceived of as a unity of elements using similar and recurring decorative patterns. Additions to preexisting services were frequently made either to replace lost pieces or to enlarge an original set. Hillwood's set of plates and ice cups dating from 1768 (fig. 51) may have had additions made as late as ten years later, for a diamond-shaped tray with the same decorative pattern was made in 1778 (fig. 52).

Elements of the table service were also established at this time. The number of shapes needed was determined by dining habits. The mode in eighteenth-century France was to dine *à la française*. This meant that dishes, instead of being served individually to each diner, were set on the table according to a preestablished order. Diners then helped themselves to the various dishes. Successive courses, varying from three to eight, were served in this manner. Between each course the table was totally cleared, with the exception of the centerpiece.

A dinner, for example, might consist of a first course with *terrines* and *oilles*. The word *oille* derives from the Spanish *olla*, a sort of rich stew made with all kinds of meats and vegetables. It was introduced to the French

FIG. 51
PLATES AND ICE CUP FROM A 1768 SERVICE
Plates (24.45) marked with crossed letters *L* with date letter *P* for 1768,
and mark of painter Jean-Jacques Pierre *le jeune*; Dia. 9¾ in. (25 cm)
Ice cup (24.63) with date letter *P* for 1768
and mark of painter Jacques-François Micaud *père*; H. 2⅝ in. (6.6 cm)

court when Louis XIV married Marie Thérèse of Austria, daughter of Philip IV of Spain. From that time on, most services included a *pot à oille*. The shape of the *pot à oille "du roi"* (figs. 2,8) is ascribed to the creative genius of Jean-Claude Duplessis, a goldsmith and bronzemaker who was hired as artistic director and chief designer for the porcelain factory in 1745. The general outline of the tureen and platter reflects Duplessis's training as a silversmith and his sensibility in designing porcelain models. If the shape of the tureen and platter are reminiscent of the work of the great silversmiths of the period, the treatment of the surface, however, is quite different. The elaborately chased, cast, and applied volumes typically associated with silver tureens have been significantly—and effectively—reduced in their translation into porcelain. The shape is connected with the Louis XV Service, the first full-scale service made at Vincennes. Many of the new shapes that were first conceived for this royal service were continually used for tableware.[17] This piece's decoration was most likely carried out by J. B. E. Genest, the factory's chief painter who would have been responsible for decorating the most important pieces, including those destined for the *service du roi*.

Tureens were the most expensive part of a service, and for that reason they were sometimes sold separately. A pair of hard-paste tureens with pastoral trophies (figs. 53, 54) was designed in the neoclassical style and painted by a highly accomplished artist, possibly Nicolas Sinsson. The gilder Vincent masterfully completed the gilding, which is thick and shiny but untooled. Other tureens closely related to the Hillwood pair were produced as single items and presented as important diplomatic gifts, and it is

FIG. 52
DIAMOND-SHAPED DISH
(plateau "losange corbeille à jour")
Marked with crossed letters *L* enclosing date letter *AA* for 1778,
and mark of painter Jacques-François Micaud *père*
H. 9¹³⁄₁₆ in. (25 cm), W. 11¹³⁄₁₆ in. (30 cm); 24.16.2
This dish is a later addition to the ice cup and plates dating from 1768 (see fig. 51, p. 75)

quite likely that the Hillwood pair was also intended for this purpose. In 1777 two tureens and two *terrines* (the difference being that *terrines* are oval in shape rather than round) were given by Louis XVI to Joseph II, Regent of the Holy Roman Empire (they are now at the Hofburg in Vienna). Seven years later the king presented to Gustav III of Sweden two tureens almost identical to the pair given to Joseph II. (One of the Swedish ter-rines is now in the Metropolitan Museum of Art in New York.) The Hillwood tureens reportedly were a gift from Louis XVI to the duc de Montpensier, from whom they descended to the marquis de Montboissier. At some point the marks were intentionally effaced and the image ren-dered almost illegible, except for the mark of the gilder Vincent and a ghost image of a date letter, possibly *ff* for 1783.

The second course of an eighteenth-century meal consisted mainly of meats, game, and seafood. The third ordinarily contained side dishes, or *entremets,* roasts, and salads; the fourth course offered more *entremets,* veg-etables, and pies; and finally the dessert course included mainly fresh white cheese, custards, compotes, fruits, ice creams, and sorbets. In its number of pieces and variety of shapes, the so-called Morgan Service at Hillwood conforms to the standards of an average eighteenth-century French dinner service intended for twenty-four to twenty-eight diners: soup plates, din-ner plates, round dishes, shell-shaped dishes, a salad bowl, ice cups, footed dishes, ice pails, jam pots, and wine glass coolers (fig. 55). The distinct bright blue color with a touch of violet is called *bleu Fallot*. This color, as

FIG. 53
SOUP TUREEN AND TRAY
(pot à oglio "à olives" et son plateau); 24.134.3–.5

FIG. 54
PAIR TO TUREEN AND TRAY
Both tureens and trays marked with ghost of crossed letters *L* surmounted by a crown indicating hard-paste porcelain, and a partially legible mark, possibly date letter *ff* for 1783; mark of gilder Henry-François Vincent *le jeune* in gold; painting attributed to Nicolas Sinsson
24.134.1–.2, 24.134.6

Tureens: each H. 13 in. (33 cm); trays: each W. 21 in. (53.3 cm)

FIG. 55
(left)
GROUP OF MORGAN SERVICE WARES
Date marks for 1769 and 1771, and marks of painters Nicolas Catrice, Guillaume Noël,
Jean-Etienne Le Bel *l'aîné,* Edmé-François Bouillat *père,* Claude Couturier,
and Jean-Jacques Pierre *le jeune* are represented in this service.
The following shapes are illustrated (clockwise): plate *(assiette "à palmes"),* soup plate *(assiette à
potage),* wine glass cooler *(seau crénélé),* ice cups *(tasses à glace),* footed tray *(soucoupe à pied),* square
dish *(compotier carré),* two jam pots with attached tray *(plateau à deux pots de confiture),*
ice pail *(seau à glace),* salad bowl *(saladier),* and shell-shaped dish *(compotier "coquille");* 24.149

FIG. 56
(top)
ICE CUP
(tasse à glace), ca. 1778/1779
Marked with crossed letters *L*
H. 3½ in. (9 cm); 24.64
From the Cameo Service commissioned by Catherine II of Russia.

[81]

FIG. 57
SAMPLE PLATE
(assiette échantillon)
Marked with crossed letters *L* enclosing date letter *FF* for 1783,
and marks of painter François-Marie Barrat and gilder Henry-Martin Prévost
Dia. 9½ in. (24 cm); 24.108

well as this type of decoration known as *incrusté*, in which the ground color was scraped away to leave space for the flower painting, was utilized for a short period, from 1766 to 1771. Many other pieces would also have been included in large services. For example, the importance of the three principal spices in cooking—pepper, nutmeg, and cinnamon—called for the creation of tripartite condiment dishes (fig. 5) that were scattered around the *surtout* until they were removed for the dessert course.

The shapes of many utilitarian wares, such as service pieces, continued to be produced up to the time of the French Revolution and beyond. Conservatism dominated the designs of shapes for the table, yet innovative forms were created on demand, as was done for the service made for Catherine II of Russia in 1778. Produced at enormous cost, the service included new shapes based on Greek and Roman models and cameo reproductions (fig. 56).

Although plates formed part of table services, on a few occasions some were painted for display. One plate (fig. 57), part of a special group produced in 1782–83, is characterized by its unusual ground colors, unique patterns, and finely executed painting in conjunction with thickly applied and minutely tooled gold decoration. This is one of the few examples described in factory records as *assiettes d'échantillon* (sample plates).[18]

THE REVOLUTION AND THE ESTABLISHMENT OF THE Republic marked the end of royal patronage of the Sèvres factory. During the French Revolution, the factory endured a chaotic period during which politics created a divisive workplace clouded by suspicion. In 1789 production decreased by a third. The next year managers raised the question of selling the factory to pay its debts, but Louis XVI decided to keep it running at his own expense. The successful operation of Sèvres was extremely important to him, as it had been to his grandfather Louis XV. Even when his own death was imminent, Louis XVI continued to organize the annual Sèvres exhibition. The last one was held in 1792–93 at the Louvre, twelve days before the king's execution. In February 1793 the accountant at the Sèvres factory asked to whom he should submit the bill for purchases made by "Louis Capet" before his death. The king loved his factory until the end.

After the fall of the monarchy in 1793, the National Convention decided that the factory, "one of the glories of France," should be preserved rather than disposed along with other royal holdings. At this time of upheaval, the factory certainly could not depend on royal commissions and purchases from the French aristocracy. Efforts were concentrated on attracting French and foreign dealers who would sell the porcelains abroad. The yellow service with birds and "Etruscan" borders was one such service sold to a dealer for export (fig. 58). Its austere decoration reflected the republican spirit of the times. Both soft-paste and hard-paste porcelains

Fig. 58
GROUP OF WARES
From a yellow service with "Etruscan" borders, 1774
Birds derived from Buffon's *Histoire Naturelle des Oiseaux*
Marked with *Sèvres* and *R. F.* (for Republique Française), and marks of painters Edmé-François
Bouillat *père*, Jean-Pierre Fumez, Jean-Baptiste Tandart *l'aîné*, Pierre Massy, Etienne Evans,
and gilder Pierre-Jean-Baptiste Vandé *fils*; 24.130
Each piece is inscribed on the back with the name of the bird represented on the front.

were used for this service. This mix may indicate that leftover soft-paste white ware was rescued and some hard-paste porcelain was added to complete the service. In these turbulent years the need to economize took priority. Royal marks and Revolutionary marks both appear in this service. By order of the National Convention, in 1793 a mark reading *Sèvres* and the initials *R. F.* (for Republique Française) replaced the royal cipher. The coexistence of these two marking systems may be explained by the fact that a complete change of marks might jeopardize sales abroad as foreigners were accustomed to the old marks. Since the Revolution was mostly an internal matter, or so it was thought, it is not surprising that for export purposes, commercial interests came first.

In a similar way, a cup and saucer with armorial decoration (fig. 59) date to the years when, at the height of the Jacobin power during the Reign of Terror, it would have been unthinkable to create such a service for the

FIG. 59
CUP AND SAUCER
(gobelet "litron" et soucoupe) with arms of Prince Bariatinskii
Marked with crossed letters *L* with date letter *qq* for year 1794
in the Ancien Régime marking system
Cup H. 2⁵/₁₆ in. (6 cm); saucer Dia. 4¹¹/₁₆ in. (12 cm); 24.40.1–.2

French market. Far from having been produced for a French aristocrat, this cup and saucer formed part of a large service that was sent to St. Petersburg in 1794. All the pieces bore the arms of Prince Bariatinskii, the former Russian ambassador to the court of Versailles who had acted as an intermediary in the commission of the Cameo Service for Catherine II.

For the domestic market, a parallel production existed for the creation of pieces imbued with the French republican spirit. Numerous wares painted with allegorical symbols of Liberty, Equality, and Reason, as well as Masonic symbols and emblems extolling republican virtues, were sold (fig. 60). In 1794 a dealer observed that the "employees have received orders not to let any piece out before putting the attributes of liberty on it. This measure might be good for the nation, but if it continues to be applied to every object, it will become impossible to export them, because this type of merchandise is unsalable in other countries."[19]

FIG. 60
CUP AND SAUCER WITH REVOLUTIONARY SYMBOLS
(gobelet "litron" et soucoupe)
Marked *Sèvres* and *R. F.* (for Republique Française), and date letter *qq* for year 1794
in the Ancien Régime marking system
Also marks of painter Jacques-François-Louis de Laroche and gilder Henry-Martin Prévost
Cup H. 3⁵/₁₆ in. (5.9 cm); saucer Dia. 4¾ in. (12 cm); 24.159.1–.2

The Creative Genius of Alexandre Brongniart

During Alexandre Brongniart's tenure as director of the factory (1800–47), Sèvres enjoyed a period of refreshing reinvigoration. Brongniart's insatiable search for new porcelain techniques and his flair for innovative decoration are well reflected in two examples at Hillwood produced during the reign of Charles X. The *Oiseaux de l'Amérique Méridionale* Service stands out as a prime example of the freshness and creativity that came to characterize Sèvres productions during the Restoration (figs. 62–64). To decorate this dessert service Brongniart called upon Madame Knip (née Pauline de Courcelles) to paint the striking series of birds featured on every piece. Rather than adapt the birds from books, as had been a customary practice in the eighteenth century, Madame Knip accompanied Brongniart to the Musée d'Histoire Naturelle, where they selected the species that she then drew for the service. C. F. J. Leloi composed the border ornaments based on South American flora from each bird's natural habitat. They were then painted by Durosey. Each plate is inscribed with the scientific name of the bird on the front. From conception to completion, the service took three years to produce. By order of King Charles X, this service was delivered in 1826 to the duchesse d'Angoulême, the only surviving daughter of Louis XVI and Marie Antoinette.

A large vase with birds (figs. 61, 65) was decorated much in the same spirit. The vase was one of three made for presentation at the 1822–23 annual exhibition at the Louvre. These annual exhibitions of new creations

Fig. 61

Bird painting by Madame Knip (detail of fig. 65, p. 93)

FIG. 62
PLATE
From the *Oiseaux de l'Amérique Méridionale* Service
Inscribed *Le Ministre* on front and *Pne. Fme. de Courcelles / Mme. Knip* below; back marked with
crossed letters *L* enclosing a fleur-de-lys (monogram of Louis XVIII),
and *Sèvres 20* printed in blue, letters *Y* and *N.* in gold, and *26.11 gbre, no. 54* in black
Dia. 9¼ in. (23.5 cm); 24.136.4

FIG. 63
SUGAR BOWL WITH TRAY *(sucrier "Mèlissin")*
From the *Oiseaux de l'Amérique Méridionale* Service
Bowl and tray marked with crossed letters *L* enclosing a fleur-de-lys (monogram of Louis XVIII),
and *Sèvres 20*, all printed in blue; *M.V. C, 15 Juillet* below in gold, and *D.Y.* in red
Tray L. 9½ in. (23.5 cm); bowl H. 4½ in. (11 cm), L. 10 in. (25.5 cm); 24.136.11–13

FIG. 64
COMPOTE *(jatte à fruits "Hemisphérique")*
From the *Oiseaux de l'Amérique Méridionale* Service
Marked with crossed letters *L* enclosing a fleur-de-lys (monogram of Louis XVII), and *Sèvres 20*,
all printed in blue; *2-81, Mc 24 Debre 1819*, and *D.Y.* painted in gold; *no. 7-no. 8* painted in black
Dia. 7⁹/₁₆ in. (19 cm); H. 4¹³/₁₆ in. (12 cm); 24.136.16

from Sèvres had been canceled during the Revolution. With the restoration of the Bourbon monarchy, Louis XVIII and Charles X, brothers of the late Louis XVI, continued the tradition of exhibiting the latest creations of the royal porcelain works. This vase with luscious floral swags, colorful birds, lavish anthemion, and garlands of grain resulted from the creative collaboration of Brongniart as project coordinator, Evariste Fragonard as the designer of the shape (known as *vase "floréal"*), Madame Knip as the bird painter, Didier as the painter of ornaments, and Boullemier the elder as the gilder.

FIG. 65
VASE WITH AFRICAN BIRDS
(vase "floréal"), 1822
Marked with crossed letters *L* enclosing a fleur-de-lys (monogram of Louis XVIII)
H. 28 in. (71 cm); 24.81
*The vase was designed by Evariste Fragonard, the birds were painted by Madame Knip,
the ornaments were created by Didier, and the gilding was the work of Boullemier l'aîné.*

A WORD ABOUT FAKES

THE NUMBER OF *FAUX SÈVRES* IS STAGGERING. NO COLLECtion is without its share of forgeries, and Hillwood's is no exception. Some factory decisions made in the early nineteenth century resulted in unmeasurable consequences in regard to fakes. When Alexandre Brongniart became director in 1800, he deemed it necessary to improve the cash flow and to clear storage areas of leftover stock of old-fashioned shapes and rejects (that is, faulty pieces) that had been collecting dust in their undecorated state. He solved his monetary and space problems by selling off unused white wares. Brongniart could not foresee the unfortunate consequences of this decision. Decorators and dealers bought these blanks by the wagonload and proceeded to decorate them in the Sèvres manner, often giving them spurious marks to deceive the public even further. Two other massive sales of undecorated stock took place in 1826 and 1840.

Many tablewares that were simply decorated with sprigs of flowers on a white ground flooded the market following the Napoleonic Wars. Agents in Paris sent them off to dealers in London. Once there, the decoration was rubbed off by immersing pieces in fluoric acid, which completely destroyed the glaze and the enamel colors. Pieces were then richly redecorated with busy, old Sèvres patterns and overly fussy gilding. As early as the 1840s confusion between real Sèvres pieces and counterfeits was well established. The spread of misinformation about the history of the factory only added to the problem. When the countess of Blessington visited Paris

FIG. 66
PART OF A "CABBAGE LEAVES" PATTERN SERVICE
In turquoise blue, with reserves painted with birds, flowers, and fruit; 24.138
While the soft-paste porcelain is genuine Sèvres, the decoration dates to circa 1840 and is possibly English.
The pieces of this large service feature a wide variety of painters and date marks
from 1761 to the years of the Republic.

in the 1841, she vividly recalled, "I have spent, or lost, a great part of the day visiting the *marchands de curiosités* in the quai de Voltaire, and left with a lighter purse than when I first walked in. In my opinion, it is impossible to resist the exquisite porcelains of Sèvres, which the genteel women of the reign of Louis XIV used in their banquets, or those they use for their floral arrangements or for their pots-pourris."[20] Not only did she have the dates of the factory wrong, but it is also quite likely that much of the Sèvres she saw was redecorated.

Other types of forgeries were not painted on genuine Sèvres paste wares but were mainly created at Tournai in Belgium and at Saint-Amand-les-Eaux. In 1877 Lady Charlotte Schreiber noted in her journal that she saw at Tournai "a quantity of pure white vases of old Sèvres forms, which go to Paris and are there decorated by the dealers and are sold for fine and genuine 'vieux' Sèvres."[21] In that same year she visited Monsieur Bettignie's works at Saint-Amand-les-Eaux, where "[Monsieur Bettignie] first took us to see his rooms full of finished pottery and porcelain, the latter consists of white pieces, 'pâte tendre' copied from the old Sèvres, which he told us was bought by dealers in Paris to be there painted and sold as old."[22] Later in Paris, Lady Schreiber encountered the redecorated Sèvres at the shop of Monsieur A. Lehujeur in the faubourg Saint-Martin. "We saw a vast number of copies of Sèvres, which were very pretty, but could not deceive the amateur, I should think."[23]

Although some fakes at Hillwood were passed to Mrs. Post as genuine, most of the later decorated Sèvres pieces are part of tablewares that Mrs. Post consciously bought to use on her dining room table. A service she acquired in 1953, to which she added in 1954, was described in the bill of sale as an "old Sèvres dessert service painted with birds in landscapes in natural colors on white ground, enclosed in turquoise blue borders." It was labeled as maker unknown, circa 1820 (fig. 66). In fact, the decoration can be identified as the work of John Randall, who between 1800 and 1850 decorated porcelain with birds in the Sèvres style for many factories, including the Coalport factory, the small Madeley factory in Shropshire, and the Welsh factories of Swansea and Nantgarw. Much of it was decorated for Edward Baldock, a London retailer known for his "Baldock Sèvres."

The redecoration of Sèvres wares and the production of fakes in the nineteenth century give testimony to the enormous and continuing popularity of shapes and decorations produced by Sèvres in the previous century. Indeed, the fascination continued into the early twentieth century. For Mrs. Post and other discerning collectors, Sèvres epitomized the good taste and grandeur of a bygone era.

Appendix of Artists' Marks

FRANÇOIS-MARIE BARRAT, painter of flowers, fruits, and *cartels historiés* (1761–91)

EDMÉ-FRANÇOIS BOUILLAT *père,* painter of flowers (1758–1810)

CHARLES-NICOLAS BUTEUX *l'aîné,* painter of attributes and trophies (1756–82)

PHILIPPE CASTEL, painter of landscapes and birds (1772–96)

NICOLAS CATRICE, painter of flowers and garlands (1757–74)

ETIENNE-JEAN CHABRY *fils,* painter of pastoral scenes (1765–87)

ANTOINE-JOSEPH CHAPPUIS *l'aîné,* painter of flowers, birds, and landscapes (1761–87)

MICHEL-BARNABÉ CHAUVAUX *l'aîné,* gilder (1753–88)

CLAUDE COUTURIER, painter of flowers (1762–75)

CHARLES-CHRISTIAN-MARIE DUROSEY, gilder (1802–30)

NICOLAS DUTANDA, painter of flowers and arabesques (1765–1802)

ETIENNE EVANS, painter of birds, landscapes and flowers (1752–75, 1778–1806)

JEAN-PIERRE FUMEZ, painter of flowers and ornaments (1778–1804)

Attributed to JEAN-BAPTISTE-ETIENNE GENEST, head of painter's studio (1752–89)

Attributed to EDMÉ GOMERY, painter (1756–58)

JACQUES-FRANÇOIS-LOUIS DE LAROCHE, painter of flowers, garlands, and bouquets (1760–1802)

JEAN-ETIENNE LE BEL *l'aîné*, painter of flowers and figures (1767–75)

ETIENNE-HENRY LE GUAY, gilder (1748–49, 1751–96)

DENIS LEVÉ, painter of flowers and birds (1754–1805)

PIERRE MASSY, painter of flowers and birds (1778–1802)

PIERRE-ANTOINE MÉREAUD *l'aîné*, painter of flowers and borders (1754–88) and gilder (1790–91)

CHARLES-LOUIS MÉREAUD *le jeune*, painter of flowers and garlands (1756–80)

JACQUES-FRANÇOIS MICAUD *père*, painter of flowers and ornaments (1757–1810)

PIERRE-LOUIS MICAUD *fils*, painter and gilder of ornaments (1795–1834)

Attributed to FRANÇOIS MIREY, gilder (1788–91)

JEAN-LOUIS MORIN, painter of figures, flowers, marine scenes, and military subjects (1754–87)

GUILLAUME NOËL, painter of figures, flowers, and ornaments (1755–1800)

PHILIPPE PARPETTE, painter and gilder of flowers (1755–57, 1773–1800)

JEAN-JACQUES PIERRE *le jeune*, painter of flowers (1763–1800)

HENRY-MARTIN PRÉVOST, gilder (1757–97)

PIERRE-JOSEPH ROSSET *l'aîné*, painter of flowers and landscapes (1753–99)

NICOLAS SINSSON, painter of flowers and garlands (1773–95)

VINCENT TAILLANDIER, painter of flowers and small objects (1753–90)

JEAN-BAPTISTE TANDART *le jeune,* painter of fruits and flowers (1754–1803)

LOUIS-JEAN THÉVENET *père*, painter (1771–78)

THÉODORE (PIERRE-THÉODORE BUTEUX), painter and gilder (ca. 1765–84)

PIERRE-JEAN-BAPTISTE VANDÉ *fils*, gilder (1779–1824)

HENRY-FRANÇOIS VINCENT *le jeune*, gilder (1753–1806)

Notes

1. Edith Wharton and Ogden Codman, Jr., *The Decoration of Houses* (New York, 1901), p. 187.

2. Letter in Hillwood's curatorial files.

3. Ibid.

4. Ibid. (24.134).

5. Ibid., letter dated 18 March 1968.

6. "La diversité des goûts est l'ange tutelaire d'une manufacture qui roule sur des objets d'agrément: ce qui ne plaît aux uns plaît aux autres. Que l'on fuie le lourd et le trivial, qu'on donne du léger, du fin, du neuf et du varié, le succès est assuré. . . . Gentillesse, nouveauté, variété, doivent être sa devise. . . . Qui dit gentillesse dit choses légères. On ne lui demande que des éternuments de son génie semblables à ceux d'une jolie femme: c'est à dire riants et agréables." Quoted from W. B. Honey, *French Porcelain of the Eighteenth Century* (London, 1950), p. 32.

7. Xavier de Chavagnac and Gaston de Grollier, *Histoire des Manufactures Françaises de Porcelaine* (Paris, 1906), p. 172.

8. A note from volume 4 of *Memoirs des Manufactures Françaises de Porcelaine* (p. 65) attests to the determination of the royal mistress to support the porcelain factory. Quoted from *Decorative Art from the Samuel H. Kress Collection at the Metropolitan Museum of Art* (London, 1964), p. 175.

9. Geoffrey de Bellaigue, "A Diplomatic Gift," *Connoisseur* 195, no. 784 (June 1977), p. 94.

10. See Rosalind Savill, "Cameo Fever: Six Pieces from the Porcelain Dinner Service Made for Catherine II of Russia," *Apollo* 116, no. 249 (November 1982), pp. 304–11.

11. Quoted from Simon Schama, *Citizens: A Chronicle of the French Revolution* (New York, 1989), p. 43.

12. "Le Roi a commandé à la manufacture de Vincennes les fleurs de porcelaine peintes au natural avec leurs vases pour plus de huit cent mille livres, pour toutes ses maisons de campagne et spécialement pour le château de Bellevue de la marquise de Pompadour. On ne parle que de cela dans Paris, et véritablement ce luxe scandalise beaucoup." Quoted from Pierre Verlet, *Sèvres* (Paris, 1954), p. 24.

13. "Xbre 1758. Vente au comptant faite à Versailles. . . . A Monseigneur le duc d'Orléans . . . une cuvette Mahon roze 480 l[ivres]." In the Sèvres archives, registre Vy 3, f 9.

14. "Comme tout le monde: il était brûlant, je le versai par petites parties de ma tasse dans ma soucoupe." In *Tresors sur Table* (Brussels, 1984), p. 207.

15. See Rosalind Savill, *The Wallace Collection*, vol. 2, *Catalogue of Sèvres Porcelain* (London, 1988), p. 489.

16. Quoted from Svend Eriksen, *The James A. de Rothschild Collection at Waddesdon Manor: Sèvres Porcelain* (Fribourg, 1968), p. 292.

17. Liana Paredes Arend, "Sèvres Table Ware at the Hillwood Museum," *Apollo* 143, no. 407 (January 1996), pp. 13–17.

18. Four of these plates were illustrated in Edouard Garnier, *The Soft Porcelain of Sèvres* (Paris, 1892), when they belonged to the Goode collection. The sale catalogue that complemented the dispersal of the Goode collection by Christie's on 17 July 1893 stated that these plates came from the private collection of the director of the Sèvres factory.

19. Chavagnac and Grollier, *Histoire des Manufactures,* p. 222.

20. "J'ai passé, ou perdu, une grand partie de la journée à visiter les marchands de curiosités du quai de Voltaire, et en suis sorti avec une bourse plus légère qu'en y entrant. C'est impossible de résister, du mois me semble-til, aux exquises porcelaines de Sèvres dont les dames délicates du regne de Louis XIV se servaient pour les banquets, ou dans lesquelles elle mettaient leurs bouquets, ou leurs pot-pourris." Quoted from Christophe Leribault, *Les Anglais à Paris au 19e Siècle* (Paris, 1994), p. 68.

21. *Lady Charlotte Schreiber's Journals,* vol. 2, *Confidences of a Collector of Ceramics and Antiques* (London, 1911), p. 11.

22. Ibid., p. 12.

23. Ibid., p. 16.

Selected Bibliography

Brunet, Marcelle, and Tamara Préaud. *Sèvres: Des origines à nos jours.* Fribourg: Office du Livre, 1978.

Dauterman, Carl C. *The Wrightsman Collection.* Vol. 4, *Porcelain.* New York: Metropolitan Museum of Art, 1970.

Dawson, Aileen. *French Porcelain: A Catalogue of the British Museum Collection.* London: British Museum Press, 1994.

Eriksen, Svend, and Geoffrey de Bellaigue. *Sèvres Porcelain: Vincennes and Sèvres 1740–1800.* London: Faber and Faber, 1987.

Musée du Louvre. *Un défi au goût: 50 ans de création à la manufacture royale de Sèvres (1740–1793).* Paris: Réunion des Musées Nationaux, 1997.

Préaud, Tamara, and Antoine d'Albis. *La Porcelaine de Vincennes.* Paris: Adam Biro, 1991.

Préaud, Tamara et al. *The Sèvres Porcelain Manufactory: Alexandre Brongniart and the Triumph of Art and Industry, 1800–1847.* New Haven: Yale University Press, 1997.

Sassoon, Adrian. *J. Paul Getty Museum. Vincennes and Sèvres Porcelain: Catalogue of the Collections.* Malibu, Calif.: J. Paul Getty Museum, 1991.

Savill, Rosalind. *The Wallace Collection: Catalogue of Sèvres Porcelain.* 3 vols. London: Trustees of the Wallace Collection, 1988.